CommunityDevelopment
Financial Institutions Fund

Promoting
Investment
in Distressed
Communities:

THE NEW MARKETS
TAX CREDIT PROGRAM

UNITED STATES DEPARTMENT OF THE TREASURY

PREPARED BY

Financial Strategies & Research
Office of Program and Policy
CDFI Fund, U.S. Department of the Treasury

Andrew Bershadker

James Greer

Supapol Siris

Michael Bzdil

OCTOBER 2008

Message from the Director

I am pleased to present this analysis of activities undertaken through the New Markets Tax Credit (NMTC) Program. This analysis is based upon data collected by the Community Development Financial Institutions Fund between 2002 and 2007.

In the relatively short period of time since the NMTC Program's inception, it has become an increasingly popular and critical tool for facilitating the investment of private sector capital in low-income communities. The summary findings in this report indicate that, among other things:

- NMTC investments are being made in communities with significantly higher levels of distress than are minimally required under program rules. Over 75 percent of NMTC-financed projects were located in census tracts that met one or more of the following distress criteria: 1) a poverty rate of at least 30 percent; 2) a median family income at or below 60 percent of the applicable area median family income; or 3) an unemployment rate at least 1.5 times the national average.

- There is a strong demand for tax credit allocations. The total amount requested by Community Development Entities (CDEs) since program inception is over eight times the amount of allocation authority available to be awarded.

- The NTMC Program is tremendously cost effective. As the report shows, every $1 of federal tax revenue foregone as a result of the credit is estimated to induce over $14 of investments in projects in low-income communities.

- Community Development Entities have been successful in securing investor capital. Through 2007, investors placed over $9 billion into CDEs, or approximately 75 percent of the $12.1 billion in allocation authority awarded in the first four allocation rounds.

- The NMTC Program is fostering new investor relationships. Over 76 percent of NMTC investors were not affiliated with the CDEs in which they made an investment, and over 61 percent of the dollars invested came from entities that had never before made an investment in the CDE.

- Virtually all NMTC product offerings include non-traditional rates and terms. Over 98 percent of the transactions offered preferential rates and terms to the borrowers. The most common features are below market interest rates (83 percent of transactions), lower origination fees (59 percent of transactions), and longer than standard periods of interest-only payments (54 percent of transactions).

I am encouraged by these findings and the progress of the NMTC Program to date. Investing in low-income communities involves risks, both real and perceived, that can be difficult to overcome. The NMTC Program offers an efficient and valuable means to help mitigate these risks, thus facilitating the flow of capital in underserved and often untested markets.

Table of Contents

 # Executive Summary

This report provides a descriptive summary of the New Markets Tax Credit (NMTC) program results derived from 2002-2007 data collected and maintained by the Community Development Financial Institutions Fund (CDFI Fund). As a descriptive report, it is not intended to be a critical analysis or to raise policy issues that may be informed by the findings set forth herein.

Through the NMTC Program, the CDFI Fund allocates tax credit authority to Community Development Entities (CDEs) that provide tax credits to investors; the proceeds of these investors' investments are used by the CDEs to finance business and real estate developments in low-income communities. The CDFI Fund collects annual data from CDEs, as required by an allocation agreement entered into by the allocatee. This data can be grouped into three categories, and are presented in three different sections of this report:

Section II: Application Data – This section contains an analysis of information that is collected at the time of NMTC application submission, including data provided by CDEs in their allocation applications, as well as an analysis of the scoring provided by the application reviewers.

Section III: Investor Data – This section contains an analysis of information pertaining to the characteristics of the investments that are being made into CDEs, and the types of investor entities making those investments.

Section IV: Investment Data – This section contains an analysis of data pertaining to the loans and investments made by CDEs using NMTC investment proceeds.

Key findings set forth in each of the three Sections are as follows:

Section II: Application Data

- Through five competitive application rounds from 2002-2007, the total amount of NMTC allocation authority requested by applicants ($132.4 billion) has been over eight times greater than the amount of allocation authority available for the CDFI Fund to award ($16 billion).

- In total, less than 23 percent of applicants were successful in receiving awards.

- The average award size ($59 million) was just 53 percent of the average award request ($111 million).

- CDFIs have been the most successful in securing NMTC allocations of the several kinds of entities to form CDEs and apply for allocations, including both "mission-driven" organizations (i.e., CDEs that are formed by non-profits, CDFIs, or governmental institutions) and "profit-driven" institutions (i.e., CDEs that are formed by for-profit organizations, including regulated financial institutions and publicly-traded companies).

- In the three rounds from 2005-2007, the largest percentage of applications has come from CDEs serving local service areas; however, the largest percentage of awards made during this period has been made to CDEs with a national service area.

- The percent of investments CDEs anticipate will be deployed to areas of "higher distress" has risen steadily, from an average of 77 percent in round two, to an average of 97 percent in round five.

- For the three rounds from 2005-2007, approximately 52 percent of the awards were made to CDEs that had never before received an NMTC allocation award.

Section III: Investor Data

- As of December 31, 2007, investors placed over $9 billion in CDEs, or approximately 75 percent of the $12.1 billion in NMTC allocation authority awarded through the first four allocation rounds.

- Approximately 94 percent of the NMTC allocations awarded in round 1 (2001-2), and over 86 percent of the NMTC allocations awarded in round 2 (2003-4), have been claimed by investors.

- Banks and other regulated financial institutions comprised the largest percentage (37 percent) of the NMTC investor pool.

- Over 76 percent of the investors were not affiliated with the CDE in which they made an investment, and over 61 percent of the dollars invested came from entities that had never before made an investment in the CDE.

Section IV: Investment Data

- Through the end of FY 2006, CDEs made close to $5.6 billion of investments in low-income communities.

- These investments supported over 1,100 businesses and real estate developments in 47 states, the District of Columbia, and Puerto Rico.

- Approximately 83 percent of the transactions (91 percent of the dollars) were invested in Metropolitan counties. Seventeen percent of the transactions, and just 8.5 percent of the dollars, were invested in Non-Metropolitan counties.

- Approximately 51 percent of the transactions supported real estate businesses and 49 percent of the transactions supported operating businesses. However, approximately 68 percent of the dollars was invested in real estate businesses, versus 32 percent in the operating businesses.

- The most common type of investments was term loans, which represented over 85 percent of all transactions. Equity investments were the second most common structure, representing approximately 10 percent of the transactions.

- Over 98 percent of all transactions offered preferential rates and terms to the borrowers/investees. The most common features were below-market interest rates (83 percent of transactions) and lower origination fees (59 percent of transactions).

- The below market-rate loans made to operating businesses were, on average, over 400 basis points lower than the market-rate loans made to operating businesses; and the below market-rate loans made to real estate businesses were, on average, over 200 basis points lower than the market-rate loans made to real estate businesses.

- Approximately 95 percent of the projects financed with NMTCs were located in designated areas of higher economic distress. Over 75 percent of projects were located in census tracts with: 1) a poverty rate of at least 30 percent; 2) a median family income at or below 60 percent of the applicable area median family income; or 3) an unemployment rate at least 1.5 times the national average.

- CDEs reported that 466 of the real estate projects funded with NMTC proceeds created construction jobs, with a median of 80 jobs created; 320 of said real estate projects created jobs at the tenant businesses, with a median of 80 jobs created or maintained; and 233 of the operating businesses created or maintained a median of 16 full-time employees (FTEs).

- On average, each $1 of NMTC investment supported total project costs totaling $3.56.

- Every $1 of federal tax revenue foregone as a result of the NMTC Program is estimated to induce over $14 of investments in projects in low-income communities.

Introduction:
The New Markets Tax Credit Program

The NMTC Program was initially authorized through the Community Renewal Tax Relief Act of 2000[1]. The NMTC Program facilitates investment in low-income communities by permitting taxpayers to receive a credit against Federal income taxes for making Qualified Equity Investments (QEIs) in designated Community Development Entities (CDEs). Substantially all of these QEI dollars must in turn be used by the CDE to provide Qualified Low Income Community Investments (QLICIs), which principally consist of investments in businesses and real estate developments in low-income communities.

The credit provided to the investor totals 39 percent of the amount of the investment and is claimed over a seven-year credit allowance period. In each of the first three years, the investor receives a credit equal to five percent of the total amount paid for the stock or capital interest at the time of purchase. For the final four years, the value of the credit is six percent annually. Investors may not redeem their investments in CDEs prior to the conclusion of the seven-year period.

The CDFI Fund is responsible for certifying entities as CDEs and administering the competitive allocation of tax credit authority. A CDE is a domestic corporation or partnership that serves as an intermediary vehicle for the provision of loans, investments, or financial counseling to low-income communities. To qualify as a CDE, an entity must: 1) have a mission of serving, or providing investment capital for, low-income communities or low-income persons; 2) maintain accountability to residents of low-income communities through their representation on a governing board of or an advisory board to the entity; and 3) be certified by the CDFI Fund as a CDE. Applicants may submit CDE certification applications throughout the year and are approved by the CDFI Fund on a rolling basis.

Through 2008, the CDFI Fund is authorized to allocate $19.5 billion in tax credit authority to CDEs[2]. The first allocation round took place in 2002 and as of December 31, 2007, the CDFI Fund completed five rounds in total. In these five allocation rounds, $16 billion of tax credit authority has been distributed, including $1 billion of special allocation authority to be used for the recovery and redevelopment of the Hurricane Katrina Gulf Opportunity (GO) Zone. The remaining $3.5 billion in authority will be issued to CDEs in the Fall of 2008. An additional $3.5 billion in allocation authority for 2009 has been requested by the President in the Administration's FY 2009 budget request; at the time of this publication, additional allocation authority has not been authorized by Congress.

---

[1] The Community Renewal Tax Relief Act of 2000 (Pub. L. No. 106-554) contains the original $15 billion in NMTC program authority. The Gulf Opportunity (GO) Zone Act of 2005 (Pub. L. No. 1109-135) added $1 billion in NMTC authority. Public Law No. 109-432 added $3.5 billion in GO Zone authority to the NMTC program for an additional round in 2008.

[2] The CDFI Fund does not allocate tax credits directly to CDEs or QALICBs. Rather, the CDFI Fund allocates authority to CDEs to raise equity investments for which investors may take a tax credit.

A CDE that is awarded an allocation of NMTC authority by the CDFI Fund has five years from the date of entering into an allocation agreement to obtain QEIs from its investors. The CDE then has 12 months to place "substantially all" (generally 85 percent) of the proceeds from the QEIs in QLICIs. There are four types of eligible QLICIs: 1) loans to, or investments in, Qualified Active Low-Income Community Businesses (QALICBs), which include both operating businesses and real estate developments; 2) loans to, or investments in, other CDEs; 3) the purchase of qualifying loans originated by other CDEs; and 4) financial counseling and other services (FCOS) to low-income community businesses.

NMTC allocations have been in high demand throughout the program's history, with the allocation amount requested being approximately six to ten times greater than the amount available in each round. Table 1-1 shows the application history of the NMTC Program by allocation round. On a cumulative basis, applicants have requested over eight times the amount of allocation authority available for the CDFI Fund to award CDEs.

Table I-1: Allocation History Since Program Inception (Dollars in Billions)[3]

Round	Applications		Awards	
	Number	Amount Requested	Number	Amount
1 (2001/2)	345	$25.8	66	$2.5
2 (2003/4)	265	$29.6	63	$3.5
3 (2005)	203	$22.5	41	$2.0
4 (2006)	239	$27.2	63	$4.1
5 (2007)	252	$27.4	61	$3.9
All Rounds	1,304	$132.4	294	$16.0

Please note that most of the subsequent tables do not report results for round 1 because of a lack of detailed demographic data requested in the first round for applicants and awardees.

---

[3] In rounds 2 through 5, a small number of the applications were determined to be ineligible prior to their applications being scored (6 applicants in round 2; 5 applicants in round 3; 15 applicants in round 4; and 6 applicants in round 5). These applicants are excluded from the analysis.

Application Data

This section contains an examination of types of organizations that have applied for an allocation of NMTCs, the amounts of their requests, and the proposed use of their allocations. It includes a comparison of the applicants to the successful subset that was awarded an allocation. The analysis in this section excludes the first round of applications because the CDFI Fund did not begin collecting most of its descriptive data about the applicants in a uniform fashion until the second round.

Organization Structure

The CDFI Fund requires that each applicant identify whether either it or its parent company is a for-profit, or non-profit organization, government-controlled entity, a Tribal entity, a thrift institution, bank or bank holding company, a credit union, a publicly-traded company, a Small Business Administration (SBA)-designated Small Business Investment Company (SBIC), Specialized Small Business Investment Company (SSBIC), New Markets Venture Capital Company (NMVCC), a certified CDFI, a minority-owned institution, or a faith-based institution.[4]

In any given allocation round, only a very small percentage of applicants self-report as credit unions, faith-based institutions, Tribal entities, minority-owned institutions or any of the three SBA designated companies. Thus, the analysis that follows focuses on the following four institutional groupings: non-profit entities; banks, thrifts or public traded companies; governmental entities; and CDFIs.

Table II-1a indicates, for each of rounds 2-5 and in the aggregate, the percentage of the applicant pool that comprised each of the four types of institutional groupings. On a cumulative basis through the four rounds, 36.2 percent of the applicants were non-profit entities; 22.5 percent of the applicants were banks, thrifts or publicly traded companies; 14.6 percent of the applicants were CDFIs; and 11.2 percent of the applicants were governmental entities. Governmental entities increased their application percentage each year, the only group to do so. They comprised less than 6 percent of the applicant pool in Round 2, but more than doubled to almost 15 percent in Round 5.

---

[4]Note that the organizational structures are not mutually exclusive. A bank is not only a depository institution; it is also a for-profit and may also be a publicly-traded company. A certified CDFI may be a non-profit, a credit union, and a faith-based institution. In cases where an applicant has a Controlling Entity, the organizational structure of the Controlling Entity is used to classify the CDE. For example, if the applicant is a for-profit entity controlled by a non-profit, the applicant is deemed a non-profit. Likewise, an applicant that has a Controlling Entity that is a certified CDFI is categorized as a certified CDFI.

Table II-1a: Organizational Structure of Applicants

Round	All Applicants	Thrift, Bank, or Bank Holding Company / Publicly-traded Company		Certified CDFI		Non-Profit		Government Controlled Entity	
		Number	Percent	Number	Percent	Number	Percent	Number	Percent
2	265	59	22.3%	39	14.7%	101	38.1%	15	5.7%
3	203	44	21.7%	32	15.8%	72	35.5%	24	11.8%
4	239	61	25.5%	39	16.3%	87	36.4%	31	13.0%
5	252	52	20.6%	30	11.9%	87	34.5%	37	14.7%
All	959	216	22.5%	140	14.6%	347	36.2%	107	11.2%

Note: Totals do not add to 100 percent because categories are not mutually exclusive and some institutional types are not listed.

Table II-1b indicates, for each of Rounds 2-5 and in the aggregate, the percentage of the awardee pool that comprised each of the four types of institutional groupings. By comparing the results in this table with those in Table II-1a, one can compare how certain institutional groupings fared with respect to their representation in the applicant pool. Based on this analysis, CDFIs have in the aggregate fared the best—comprising close to 20 percent of the awardee pool, compared with just 14.6 percent of the applicant pool. Thrifts, banks and publicly traded companies were also slightly over-represented in the awardee pool (25.9% vs. 22.5%), while the non-profits and governmental entities tended to receive awards generally in proportion to their representation in the applicant pool.

Table II-1b: Organizational Structure of Allocatees

Round	All Allocatees	Thrift, Bank, or Bank Holding Company / Publicly-traded Company		Certified CDFI		Non-Profit		Government Controlled Entity	
		Number	Percent	Number	Percent	Number	Percent	Number	Percent
2	63	18	28.6%	11	17.5%	23	36.5%	8	12.7%
3	41	8	19.5%	11	26.8%	17	41.5%	4	9.8%
4	63	18	28.6%	16	25.4%	24	38.1%	4	6.3%
5	61	15	24.6%	7	11.5%	17	27.9%	10	16.4%
All	228	59	25.9%	45	19.7%	81	35.5%	26	11.4%

Note: Totals do not add to 100 percent because categories are not mutually exclusive.

Table II-1c indicates, for each of Rounds 2-5 and in the aggregate, the percentage of each institutional grouping that received an award, enabling one to compare the success rate of each institutional grouping with the success rate of the entire applicant pool. For the four rounds, just under 24 percent of the

applicants received allocations. Each institutional grouping, with the exception of the non-profit entities, received allocations at a better rate than the rate of the entire applicant pool. CDFIs, with a success rate of 32.1 percent, demonstrated a significantly higher success rate than the other three institutional groupings.

Table II-1c: Success Rate by Organizational Structure

Round	All Applicants	Thrift, Bank, or Bank Holding Company / Publicly-traded Company	Certified CDFI	Non-Profit	Government Controlled Entity
	Percent	Percent	Percent	Percent	Percent
2	23.8%	30.5%	28.2%	22.8%	53.3%
3	20.2%	18.2%	34.4%	23.6%	16.7%
4	26.4%	29.5%	41.0%	27.6%	12.9%
5	24.2%	28.8%	23.3%	19.5%	27.0%
All	23.8%	27.3%	32.1%	23.3%	24.3%

CDFI Fund data permits a deeper examination of the CDFI industry's experience as NMTC Program applicants. Table II-1d shows the total number of applicants and allocatees by type of CDFI. The different CDFI institution types have experienced varying and changing levels of success in the competition for NMTC allocations. While the success rates for Depository CDFI and Loan Fund CDFI applicants across rounds 2 – 5 were similar (30.8% and 33.7%, respectively), they change considerably across rounds. Depository CDFI applicants were highly successful in the second round (3 of 5 applications, or a 60% success rate) but were significantly lower in subsequent rounds. The success rate for Loan Fund CDFIs varied noticeably across the rounds from a low of 25 percent in the second round to a high of nearly 50 percent in round 4. Applications from Venture Fund CDFIs have declined in number, and only in the second and third rounds have these applicants been successful in winning allocations.

Table II-1d. CDFI Affiliated Applicants and Allocation by Round

Round	Depository CDFIs		Loan Fund CDFIs		Venture Capital CDFIs	
	Applicants	% Awarded Allocation	Applicants	% Awarded Allocation	Applicants	% Awarded Allocation
2	5	60.0	28	25.0	6	16.7
3	7	28.6	21	33.3	4	50.0
4	8	25.0	29	48.3	2	0.0
5	6	16.7	23	26.1	1	0.0
All	26	30.8	101	33.7	13	23.1

Average Requests and Award Amounts

Table II-2 shows the average amounts requested by and awarded to different organization types and the overall average allocation amount, by round. For rounds 2 through 5 combined, the awardees' average request was approximately $111 million, and the average award size was $59 million. Banks and publicly-traded companies had the largest requests and the largest allocation amounts, on average, at $121.3 million and $70.6 million, respectively. Their highest requests ($123.6 million on average) and allocation awards were in round 4 ($85.9 million on average). Certified CDFIs generally requested and received the lowest award amounts (for rounds 2 through 5 they requested $86 million on average and received $55 million on average), but received the highest percentage of their requested amount (64%).

Table II-2. Average Allocation Award Amounts by Organization Structure and by Round (millions $)

	Thrift, Bank or Bank Holding Company / Publicly-traded Company	Certified CDFI	Government Controlled Entity	Non-Profit	All Applicants or Allocatees
Round 2					
Request	130	67.2	98.5	96.3	111.8
Award	59.7	43.9	54.0	56.4	55.6
Round 3					
Request	109.9	82.4	137.2	111.0	110.9
Award	48.6	44.9	40.0	52.4	48.8
Round 4					
Request	123.6	103.8	112.5	95.5	113.6
Award	85.9	60.8	67.3	58.6	65.1
Round 5					
Request	118.2	91.7	112.3	100.6	108.5
Award	79.0	73.9	60.8	67.8	64.1
All Rounds					
Request	121.3	86.2	116.0	99.8	111.2
Award	70.6	54.8	56.5	58.6	59.3

Areas Served

The CDFI Fund asked in the allocation application what type of geographic area the applicant proposed to serve: national, multi-state, statewide, or local. Through the allocation agreement, activities of allocatees are generally limited to the approved service areas. As shown in Table II-3, applicants and allocatees serve a range of geographic areas. (This information is not available for round 1 or round 2 applicants).

In every round, the largest percentage of applicants has been those that serve local markets. However, they represent the smallest percentage of the awardee pool. Through rounds three through five, applicants with local service areas comprised 36 percent of the applicant pool (250 out of 694), but just 21.8 percent of the awardee pool (36 out of 165). Their success rate of 14.4 percent is significantly smaller than the overall success rate of 23.8 percent. By comparison, entities serving national service areas had an overall success rate of 35.4 percent.

Table II-3: Areas Served by Applicants and Allocatees

Type of Service Area	Round	Applicants	Allocatees	Award Rate
LOCAL	3	80	13	16.3%
	4	82	10	12.2%
	5	88	13	14.8%
	Total	250	36	14.4%
STATEWIDE	3	34	8	23.5%
	4	46	9	19.6%
	5	47	11	23.4%
	Total	127	28	22%
MULTI-STATE[5]	3	32	2	6.3%
	4	49	22	44.9%
	5	44	9	20.5%
	Total	125	33	26.4%
NATIONAL	4	62	22	35.5%
	5	73	28	38.4%
	Total	192	68	35.4%
TOTALS		694	165	23.8%

---

[5] Seventeen of the allocatees serving multi-state markets in rounds 4 and 5 were GO Zone awardees that may have applied to serve a national market, but were limited to serving a multi-state market consisting of GO Zone eligible communities in Alabama, Louisiana and Mississippi.

Projected Deployment of Investments in Areas of Higher Distress

The CDFI Fund encourages applicants to commit to serving areas characterized by indicators of "higher distress."[6] Applicants are asked what percentage of their QLICIs will be devoted to such areas. Figure II-1 shows that applicants and allocatees have increasingly focused their investment efforts in areas of higher distress. On average, applicants proposed to make 81 percent of their round 2 QLICIs in areas of higher distress. By round 5, this percentage had grown to 96 percent. The average allocatee's expected percentage of QLICIs to be deployed in areas of higher distress was 77 percent in round 2; that figure increased to 90 percent in round 3 and 97 percent in round 5.

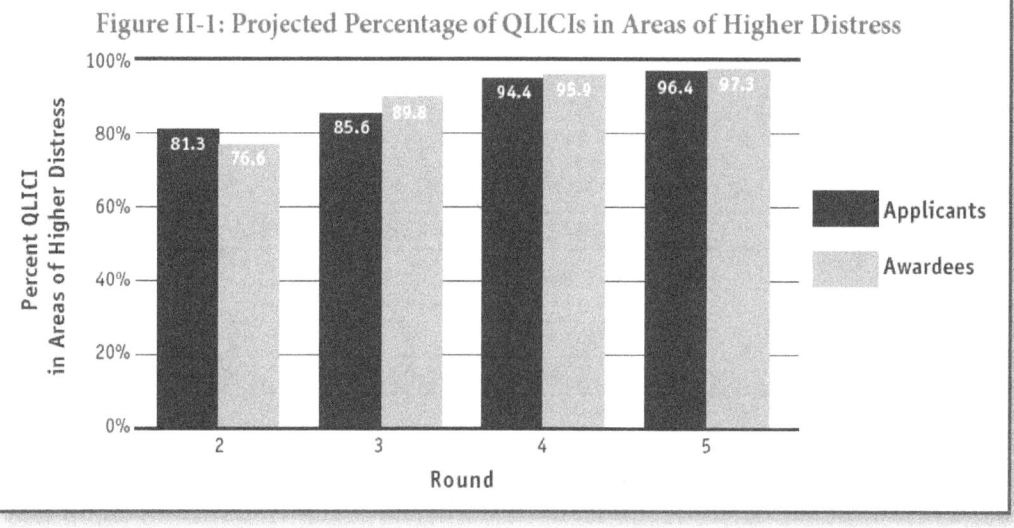

Figure II-1: Projected Percentage of QLICIs in Areas of Higher Distress

---

[6]The distress indicators have changed somewhat from round to round. For 2007 round allocatees, the distress indicators were as follows: 1) census tracts with poverty rates greater than 30%; 2) census tracts with, if located within a Non-Metropolitan area, median family income that does not exceed 60% of statewide median family income, or, if located within a Metropolitan area, median family income that does not exceed 60% of the greater of the statewide median family income or the Metropolitan area median family income; 3) census tracts with unemployment rates at least 1.5 times the national average; 4) Federally-designated Empowerment Zones, Enterprise Communities, or Renewal Communities; 5) SBA designated HUB Zones, to the extent QLICIs will support businesses that obtain HUB Zone certification by the SBA; 6) Brownfield sites as defined under 42 U.S.C. 9601(39); 7) Federally-designated medically underserved areas, to the extent QLICI activities will result in the support of health related services; 8) projects serving Targeted Populations, to the extent that: (a) such projects are located in Non-Metropolitan areas; or (b) such projects are 60% owned by low-income persons (LIPs); or (c) at least 60% of employees are LIPs; or (d) at least 60% of customers are LIPs; 9) areas encompassed by a HOPE VI redevelopment plan; 10) High Migration Rural Counties; 11) Non-Metropolitan Counties; 12) Enterprise Zone programs or other similar state/local programs targeted towards particularly economically distressed communities; 13) Counties for which the Federal Emergency Management Agency (FEMA) has: issued a "major disaster declaration" and made a determination that such County is eligible for both "individual and public assistance"; provided that the initial investment will be made within 24 months of the disaster declaration; 14) Federally designated Native American or Alaskan Native areas, Hawaiian Homelands, or redevelopment areas by the appropriate Tribal or other authority; 15) Areas designated as distressed by the Appalachian Regional Commission or Delta Regional Authority; and 16) Colonias areas, as designated by the U.S. Department of Housing and Urban Development.

Projected Deployment of Investments in Rural and Urban Areas

Applicants were asked what percentage of the allocation they proposed to deploy in major urban, minor urban and rural areas. Responses to this question were not a selection factor in the allocation award process[7]; nor were allocatees compelled by the CDFI Fund, through their allocation agreements, to invest specific amounts in such areas. Table II-4 shows the percentage allocatees expected to invest in each geographic area. Overall, the data show that allocatees anticipated that 60 percent of investments would be deployed in major urban areas, 23 percent in minor urban areas and 17 percent in rural areas.

Table II-4: Percent of Allocation to be Invested by Type of Area
Rounds 2 – 5, All Applicants

Round	Major Urban	Minor Urban	Rural
	Percentage	Percentage	Percentage
2	64%	22%	14%
3	59%	25%	16%
4	59%	23%	18%
5	57%	24%	18%
All	60%	23%	17%

Scoring of Applications

The CDFI Fund's application review process requires three reviewers to independently review and evaluate each application. The reviewers include private sector professionals with strong credentials in community development finance, Federal agency staff working in other community development finance programs, and CDFI Fund staff. Reviewers are selected on the basis of their knowledge of community and economic development finance and experience in business or real estate finance, business counseling, secondary market transactions, or financing of community-based organizations.

In scoring each application, reviewers rate each of the four evaluation sections (Business Strategy, Community Impact, Management Capacity, and Capitalization Strategy,) as follows: Weak (0-5 points); Limited (6-10 points); Average (11-15 points); Good (16-20 points); and Excellent (21-25 points). Applications can be awarded up to ten additional "priority" points for demonstrating a track record of serving disadvantaged business and communities and/or for committing to make investments in projects owned by unrelated parties.

---

[7] Starting in round 6, allocatees which indicated that they would commit to investing a portion of their allocation in "Non-Metropolitan counties" will be required to meet these minimum investment objectives through their allocation agreements.

In order to be eligible for an allocation, an application must achieve: (1) an aggregate base score (without including priority points) of at least 216 points, which approximates the middle of the Good range; and (2) an aggregate base score of at least 48 points in each of the four application evaluation criterion, which approximates the low end of the Good range.

The scores ascribed by the CDFI Fund's readers form the basis upon which allocations are awarded. For each allocation round the applicants were ranked according to a formula to achieve a rank order list of applicants. Because the CDFI Fund's tax credit authority is limited, only a portion of the applicants that meet the minimum scoring thresholds are awarded an allocation in any given round.

Figure II-2 documents the mean scores for all applicants by section by round. Across all of the review sections, scores increased with each successive round.

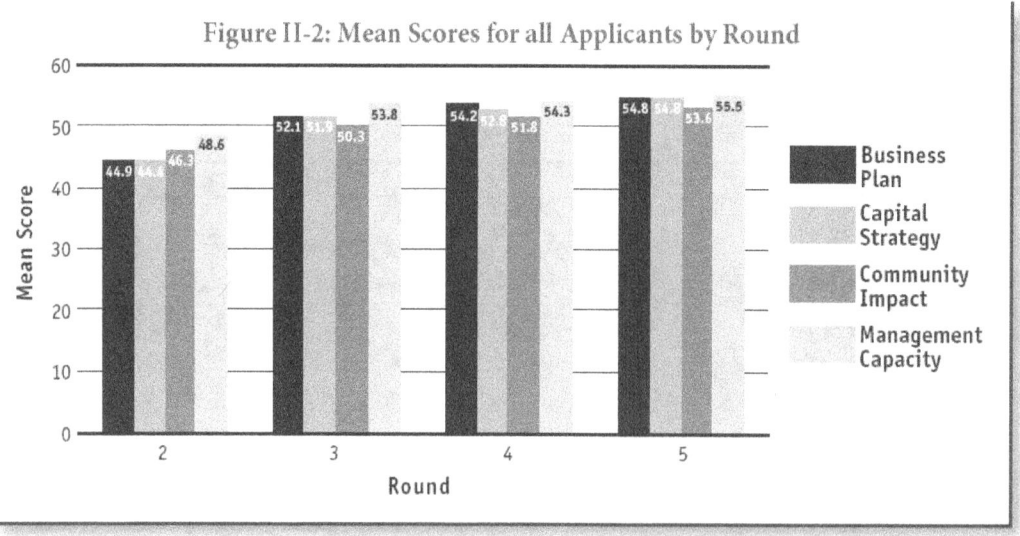

Figure II-2: Mean Scores for all Applicants by Round

Table II-5 shows additional details about the section scores. Overall, scores average in the low 50s. A means test was performed to determine if the difference of means between applicant types is statistically significant. For example: Is there a statistical difference between the scores of certified CDFIs and applicants that are not certified CDFIs? Where no statistical significance was found, it cannot be ruled out that a difference of means is the result of chance. In other words, it cannot be ruled out that a difference between groups is meaningful. In the table below, cells are marked with an asterisk to signify that the difference in means was found to be statistically significant.[8]

---

[8] A technical discussion and presentation of this data can be found in Appendix II.

The means test analysis shows that there are relatively few statistically significant differences in mean scores among application types. The analysis suggests that the application process is relatively neutral with respect to the type of applicant. There are a few exceptions. For instance, banks and publicly traded companies scored significantly above the mean in the Capitalization Strategy section in all four allocation Rounds. Similarly, CDFIs scored significantly above the mean in the Community Impact section in all four allocation rounds.

Table II-5: Mean Scores by Dimension, Round, and Organization Type

Round	Thrift, Bank, Bank Holding Company / Publicly-traded Company	Certified CDFI	Non-Profits	Government Controlled Entity	All Applicants
Mean Aggregate Business Strategy Section Score					
2	50.9*	52.0*	45.0	53.4*	44.9
3	55.2*	59.8*	52.8	52.5	52.1
4	58.6*	60.1*	55.8	53.7	54.2
5	57.4*	57.1	53.9	56.8	54.8
Mean Aggregate Capitalization Strategy Score					
2	57.6*	45.6	40.4*	50.7	44.4
3	56.2*	54.5	48.8	52.3	51.9
4	58.1*	54.0	52.3	51.7	52.8
5	60.2*	54.2	52.5	55.2	54.8
Mean Aggregate Community Impact Score					
2	49.7*	54.4*	47.5	54.2	46.3
3	49.6	57.1*	53.1	52.3	50.3
4	55.0*	58.4*	54.7*	52.7	51.8
5	55.6	58.4*	54.0	56.2	53.6
Mean Aggregate Management Capacity Score					
2	56.1*	54.6*	47.8	55.8*	48.6
3	56.5	58.7*	53.4	53.5	53.8
4	59.7*	58.5*	54.7	51.0	54.3
5	59.5*	57.9	53.8	55.6	55.5

*Indicates mean scores differences that were statistically significant at p<.05

Table II-6 shows the average scores of allocatees and non-allocatees by allocation round. In all cases allocatees scored higher than non-allocatees, but the difference in scores declined substantially in all four sections over the course of the four rounds that are analyzed.[9] For example, the mean capitalization strategy score for allocatees was over 55 percent higher than non-allocatees in round 2, but only 24 percent higher than non-allocatees in round 5. Generally, this convergence of scores is due to non-allocatees raising their scores over time, rather than allocatees being scored lower. In all four sections, non-allocatee scores jumped a particularly large amount between rounds 2 and 3.

Table II-6: Mean Scores of Allocatees vs. Non-Allocatees

Round	Allocatee		Percent
	No	Yes	Difference
Mean Aggregate Business Strategy Section Score			
2	39.8	61.1	53.4%
3	48.7	65.4	34.3%
4	50.5	64.5	27.8%
5	51.4	65.3	27.2%
Mean Aggregate Capitalization Strategy Score			
2	39.2	61.1	55.7%
3	48.9	63.9	30.6%
4	49.0	63.6	29.7%
5	51.8	64.3	24.0%
Mean Aggregate Community Impact Score			
2	41.7	61.2	47.0%
3	47.1	63.2	34.1%
4	47.9	62.8	31.2%
5	50.1	64.8	29.3%
Mean Aggregate Management Capacity Score			
2	43.6	64.5	48.0%
3	51.2	64.2	25.2%
4	50.8	64.2	26.4%
5	52.7	64.3	22.2%

---

[9] All mean score differences between allocatees and non-allocatees were statistically significant at $p < .05$.

Allocations per Allocatee

Figure II-3 shows the number of first time allocatees in each of the five allocation rounds. In the second round, 86 percent of allocatees received their first award. The percentage dropped to 66 percent in round 3, and to 49 percent and 46 percent in rounds 4 and 5 respectively. While the trend shows that repeat allocatees have been an increasing part of the allocatee pool, the number of first-time allocatees has been significant in each round.

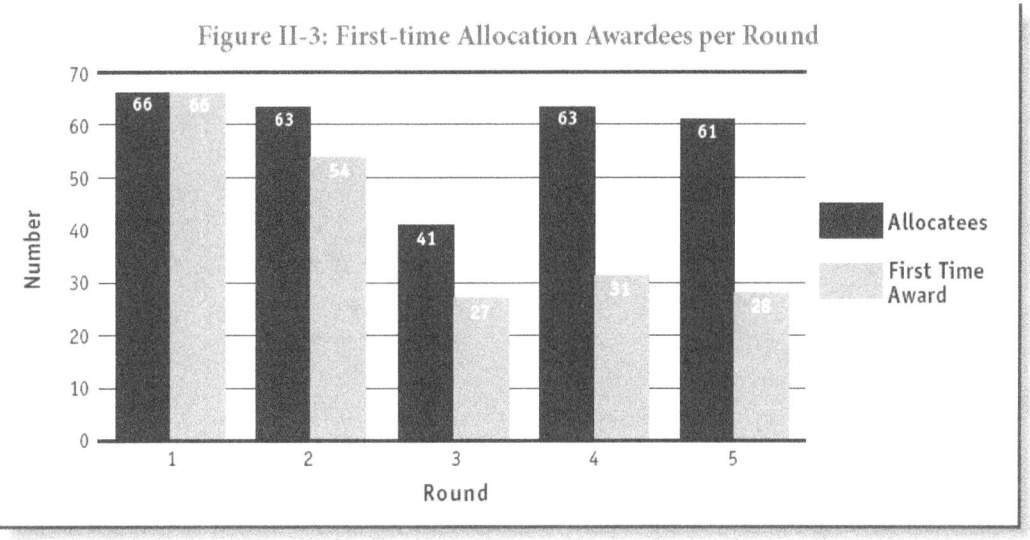

Figure II-3: First-time Allocation Awardees per Round

III. Investor Data

QEIs Through December 31, 2007

As of December 31, 2007, over $9 billion in QEIs had been issued by CDEs, representing 75 percent of the $12.1 billion of allocations issued in rounds 1 through 4. Table III-1 shows the number of allocatees and the amount of allocations made in each Round, the QEIs finalized by December 31, 2007 (both in dollar amounts and as a percentage of allocations), and the percent of allocatees that have raised any QEIs and have completed all their QEIs.[10] The first round allocatees are furthest along in raising all of their QEIs. Over $2.3 billion in QEIs had been finalized by December 31, 2007. This is 94 percent of the original NMTC allocation of $2.5 billion. Fully 97 percent of allocatees had finalized at least some of their QEIs by that date, and over 56 percent had raised all their QEIs. The raising of QEIs associated with later round awards is progressing as well. Round 4 allocatees had finalized $2.1 billion in QEIs by December 31, 2007, over half their NMTC allocation of $4.1 billion.[11] Over 87 percent of allocatees had at least begun receiving QEIs from investors and over 11 percent had completed their QEI issuance.

Table III-1. Allocations and Qualified Equity Investments (QEIs)
From Program Inception through 12/31/2007 (Rounds 1 through 4)

Allocation Round	Number of Allocatees	Amount Allocated	QEIs Raised by 12/31/2007	QEIs as a Percent of Amount Allocated	Raised 100 percent of QEIs by 12/31/2007
1	66	$2,500,000,000	$2,348,853,437	94.0%	56.1%
2	63	$3,500,000,000	$3,028,705,751	86.5%	46.0%
3	41	$2,000,000,000	$1,530,816,417	76.5%	36.6%
4	63	$4,100,000,000	$2,117,987,420	51.7%	11.1%
Total	233	$12,100,000,000	$9,026,363,025	74.6%	37.8%

[10] CDEs are required to issue all of their QEIs within five years of the CDE entering into an allocation agreement with the CDFI Fund. The CDFI Fund requires that 60 percent must be issued within three years. Round 1 allocatees were notified of their allocations on 3/14/2003. Round 2 allocatees were notified on 5/6/2004. Round 3 allocatees were notified on 5/11/2005. Round 4 allocatees were notified on 6/1/2006. Allocation agreements are typically signed within 3-6 months of award notification. Round 5 allocatees were not notified of their allocations until 10/6/07, and therefore have not been included in this analysis.

[11] Round 4 allocations include $3.5 billion in authority nationwide and an additional $600 million specifically for deployment in the Gulf Opportunity (GO) Zone.

Table III-2 presents further detail on the distribution of allocatees by percent of QEIs finalized. The table shows that 57 Round 1 allocatees (86.4 percent) have raised 75 percent or more of their QEIs, while only two (3.0 percent) have raised less than 25 percent.[12] In contrast, only 18 of the Round 4 allocatees (28.6 percent) have raised 75 percent or more of their QEIs, and 17 of the Round 4 allocatees (27.0 percent) have raised less than 25 percent of their allocation.

Table III-2. Distribution of Allocatees by Percent of QEIs Issued, by Round

Percent of QEIs Finalized	Round 1		Round 2		Round 3		Round 4	
	Allocatees	Percent	Allocatees	Percent	Allocatees	Percent	Allocatees	Percent
Less than 25.0%	2	3.0%	1	1.6%	2	4.9%	17	27.0%
25.0% to 49.9%	1	1.5%	0	0.0%	3	7.3%	9	14.3%
50.0% to 74.9%	6	9.1%	12	19.0%	12	29.3%	19	30.2%
75% or More	57	86.4%	50	79.4%	24	58.5%	18	28.6%
Total	66	100.0%	63	100.0%	41	100.0%	63	100.0%

QEIs by Investor Type

Table III-3 shows the types of investors that have made equity investments in CDEs. The table shows that the $9 billion in QEIs were largely provided through investor leveraged funds (47 percent of the QEI dollar total), with banks or other regulated financial institutions the second largest source of financing (nearly 32 percent). Overall, 2,600 investors provided an average investment of $3.4 million for QEIs finalized by December 31, 2007.

Many CDEs are choosing to secure QEIs through a leveraged structure called a "Leveraged Fund" which accounts for why the largest number and percentage share of investments shown in Table III-3 falls under that category of investor type. In a leveraged structure, the QEI investment can be leveraged with debt provided to the fund – thus enhancing the tax credit flows to the equity investors in the fund. In these instances, the ultimate "NMTC claimants" are not the leveraged fund that made the QEIs, but rather the equity investors in the fund.

---

[12] Two CDEs from round 1 that were unable to issue 60% of their QEIs within three years, so the CDFI Fund rescinded their allocation awards (totaling $9 million) and re-allocated the amounts in round 5.

Table III-3. QEIs by Investor Type (through 12/31/2007)

Investor Type	Number of Investors	Percent of Investors	$ Amount of QEIs Issued (Finalized)	Percentage of QEIs Issued (Finalized)	Average QEI
Bank or Other Regulated Financial Institution	639	24.58%	$2,900,771,873	32.14%	$4,539,549
Foundation or Other Philanthropic Organization	1	0.04%	$1,212	0.00%	$1,212
Individual Investor	25	0.96%	$53,546,613	0.59%	$2,141,865
Insurance Company	12	0.46%	$16,618,445	0.18%	$1,384,870
Investment Bank	548	21.08%	$582,387,250	6.45%	$1,062,750
Leveraged Fund	1,047	40.27%	$4,215,929,599	46.71%	$4,026,676
Other Type of Investor	188	7.23%	$720,400,197	7.98%	$3,831,916
Pension Fund	6	0.23%	$800,000	0.01%	$133,333
Real Estate Developer or Investment Company	123	4.73%	$533,582,050	5.91%	$4,338,065
Utility Company	10	0.38%	$2,075,787	0.02%	$207,579
Venture Fund	1	0.04%	$250,000	0.00%	$250,000
Total	2,600	100.00%	$9,026,363,026	100.00%	$3,471,678

Table III-4 describes the characteristics of all NMTC claimants, whether QEI investors in a traditional investment structure, or the equity investors in a leveraged fund. Tables III-5 and III-6 show the percentages of both QEIs by investors and the dollar/ amount for affiliated and new investors, respectively.

Table III-4: Characteristics of all NMTC claimants

Investor Type	Number of Investments	Percent of Investments
Bank or Other Regulated Financial Institution	1,975	37.70%
Foundation or Other Philanthropic Organization	2	0.04%
Individual Investor	1,111	21.21%
Insurance Company	243	4.64%
Investment Bank	561	10.71%
Other Type of Investor	1,202	22.94%
Pension Fund	6	0.11%
Real Estate Developer or Investment Company	125	2.39%
Utility Company	13	0.25%
Venture Fund	1	0.02%
Total	5,239	100.00%

Table III-5 shows the number, dollar amount and percentages of QEIs that were made by investors that are affiliates of the allocatee (e.g., where the QEI was provided by the allocatee's parent company).

Table III-5: QEIs By Affiliated Investors

Affiliated w/the Allocatee	# of Investors	% of Investors	$ Amount of QEIs Issued (Finalized)	% of QEIs Issued
Yes	603	23.2%	$3,280,306,957	36.3%
No	1,997	76.8%	$5,746,056,069	63.7%

Table IIII-6 shows the number, dollar amount and percentages of QEIs that were made by investors that had not previously made any investments, NMTC or otherwise, in the allocatee.

Table III-6: QEIs By New Investors

New Investor	# of Investors	% of Investors	$ Amount of QEIs Issued (Finalized)	% of QEIs Issued
Yes	1,128	43.4%	$5,525,415,931	61.2%
No	1,472	56.6%	$3,500,947,095	38.8%

Investment Data:
Analysis of Transactions and Projects

IV-1: QLICI TRANSACTION DATA

The NMTC Program statute requires CDEs to use "substantially all" (generally 85%) of the proceeds from QEIs to make Qualified Low Income Community Investments (QLICIs). Per their respective allocation agreements with the CDFI Fund, allocatees are required to file, along with their audited financial statements, Institutional Level Reports (ILR) and Transaction Level Reports (TLR) on their QLICIs using the CDFI Fund's Community Investment Impact System (CIIS). These reports are due to the CDFI Fund within six months after the end of an allocatee's fiscal year.[13] This section discusses the types of investments reported in CIIS in the two reports. It examines QLICIs made by CDEs through the end of their Fiscal Year 2006, without regard to which round the CDE received an allocation.

There are four types of QLICIs: 1) loans to, or investments in, Qualified Active Low-Income Community Businesses (QALICBs), including both operating businesses and real estate projects; 2) certain loans to, or investments in, other CDEs; 3) the purchase of qualifying loans originated by another CDE; and 4) financial counseling and other services (FCOS, generally advice to low-income community businesses).

Through the end of Fiscal Year 2006, CDEs made over 1,500 QLICIs totaling over $5.56 billion. Table IV-1 shows that $5.36 billion of QLICIs (over 94 percent) were direct investments in QALICBs. An additional $86.7 million (1.6 percent) of QLICIs were invested in other CDEs, which in turn used those dollars to make investments in QALICBs. Just under $117 million of QLICIs were used to purchase loans from other CDEs. The remaining category of QLICI, FCOS, shows too little activity to be included in Table IV-1. Only five CDEs reported any FCOS activity. The total dollar amount is less than $1 million.

Table IV-1-1: QLICI Types
(Cumulative through 2006)

QLICI Type	Number	Percent of Transactions	Amount	Percent of Dollars
Investments in other CDEs	24	1.56%	86,722,742	1.56%
Direct investments in QALICBs	1,451	94.04%	5,361,331,522	96.35%
Loan Purchases from other CDEs	68	4.41%	116,616,248	2.10%
Total QLICIs	1,543	100.00%	5,564,670,512	100.00%

---

[13]This time-lag for data submission is the primary reason why this report includes transaction level data only through FY 2006.

In the aggregate, 1,475 different QLICIs totaling over $5.4 billion were invested in QALICBs, either directly or through intermediary CDEs. The analysis in Section IV-1 of this report focuses specifically on these 1,475 QLICIs.

Investments in Metropolitan and Non-Metropolitan Counties

The data presented in Table IV-2 shows that CDEs have focused investments heavily in counties located in Metropolitan areas (91%). In 2007, Congress directed the CDFI Fund to ensure proportional investment in Non-Metropolitan counties. In response, starting with the sixth round, the CDFI Fund will require that allocatees that express a willingness to invest in Non-Metropolitan counties meet minimum investment targets. It is the CDFI Fund's goal that, beginning with the 2008 round of allocatees, at least 20% of all QLICIs will be made in Non-Metropolitan counties.

Table IV-1-2: Investments in Metropolitan and Non-Metropolitan Counties (QLICIs)

	Number	Amount ($)	Percent
Metro Counties	1,240	4,947,481,752	90.81%
Non-Metro Counties	207	464,914,781	8.53%
No Location and/or FIPS	28	35,657,732	0.65%
Total	1,475	5,448,054,265	100.00%

Financing by QALICB Type

The CDFI Fund classifies QALICBs as either real estate businesses or non-real estate businesses. A QALICB that is a real estate business is generally a single purpose entity formed to develop or lease a specific real estate transaction. A QALICB that is a non-real estate business is an operating business (e.g. with sales, revenue, customers) whose primary business is not real-estate development, ownership or management. If a non-real estate QALICB forms a single purpose entity for the purpose of leasing property to that operating business, and an allocatee finances the single purpose entity, the CDFI Fund permits the CDE to classify the single purpose entity as either a real estate or non-real estate QALICB. Table IV-1-3 shows that while almost half the QALICB investments were to non-real estate businesses, these comprised only 32 percent of the dollar value of the investments.

Table IV-1-3: Amount of Financing by QALICB Type (Cumulative through 2006)

QALICB Type	Transactions	Percent of Transactions	Amount	Percent of Dollars
Non-Real Estate	722	48.95%	1,725,357,373	31.67%
Real Estate	753	51.05%	3,722,696,891	68.33%
Total	1,475	100.00%	5,448,054,264	100.00%

Financing by QALICB Use of Funds

Table IV-1-4 presents the purpose of the QLICIs. Commercial real estate construction and rehabilitation comprised 75 percent of the use of financing dollars. An additional 21 percent was used for business working capital while 2 percent was used for residential real estate (construction and rehabilitation). The final 2 percent was for other unclassified purposes. It should be noted that commercial real estate is a broad category that includes community facilities and mixed-use[14] properties.

Table IV-1-4: QLICIs by General Purpose

Purpose	Non-Real Estate QALICBs			Real Estate QALICBs		
	Number of QLICIs	Amount ($)	Average ($)	Number of QLICIs	Amount ($)	Average ($)
Business – Working Capital	492	1,073,191,023	2,181,283	17	88,237,400	5,190,435
Real Estate – Commercial	204	593,256,151	2,908,118	700	3,498,152,300	4,997,360
Real Estate – Residential	—	—	—	25	92,138,615	3,685,545
Other	26	58,910,199	2,265,777	11	44,168,576	4,015,325
Total	722	1,725,357,373	2,389,692	753	3,722,696,891	4,943,821

Table IV-1-5 expands on Table IV-1-4 and shows the number, dollar amounts, percents, and averages of QALICB investments by use of funds. The data shows that the overwhelming amount of investment has been for real estate, including commercial and residential new construction and rehabilitation. Commercial real estate investments are almost two times larger on average than business working capital investments.

---

[14] To be eligible for NMTC financing, at least 20% of a mixed used property's annual gross revenue must be generated from commercial rents.

Table IV-1-5: Amount of Financing by Use of Funds
(Cumulative through 2006)

	N (QLICIs)	Amount ($)	Percent	Average ($)
Business – Working Capital	509	1,161,428,423	21.31%	2,281,785
Real Estate – Commercial	904	4,091,408,452	75.09%	4,525,894
Real Estate – Residential	25	92,138,615	1.69%	3,685,545
Other	37	103,078,775	1.89%	2,785,913
Total	1,475	5,448,054,264	100.00%	3,693,596

CDE investment patterns differ in Metropolitan counties and Non-Metropolitan counties. Table IV-1-6 shows financing by QALICB use of funds, separately for Metropolitan and Non-Metropolitan counties.[15] There are differences, however, in the purpose of financing between Metropolitan and Non-Metropolitan areas. Almost 70 percent of transactions and over 80 percent of dollars invested in Metropolitan counties went to commercial real estate construction or rehabilitation. An additional 27 percent of transactions, but only 15 percent of dollars, went to business working capital. In contrast, business working capital transactions dominate the purpose of financing in Non-Metropolitan counties, both in number and in dollar amount. Over 81 percent of transactions and almost 85 percent of dollars were used for this purpose.

Table IV-1-6: Financing by Purpose in Metropolitan/
Non-Metropolitan Counties

	Metro			Non-Metro		
	N (QLICIs)	Amount ($)	Percent	N (QLICIs)	Amount ($)	Percent
Business – Working Capital	343	777,522,926	15.57%	166	383,905,497	84.13%
Real Estate – Commercial	871	4,026,290,597	80.65%	33	65,117,854	14.27%
Real Estate –Residential	25	92,138,615	1.84%	—	—	—
Other	28	95,791,182	1.91%	9	7,287,593	1.59%
Total	1,267	4,991,743,321	100.00%	208	456,310,944	100.00%

---

[15] Twenty-eight transactions did not provide enough information to determine Metro/Non-Metro location so are omitted here.

Financing by Transaction Type

Figure IV-1-1 shows the distribution of QLICIs by type of investment. Over 88 percent of investment dollars took the form of term loans, and 8 percent took the form of equity investments. Very small percentages of investments were convertible debt (about 2 percent) and lines of credit (about 1.3 percent).

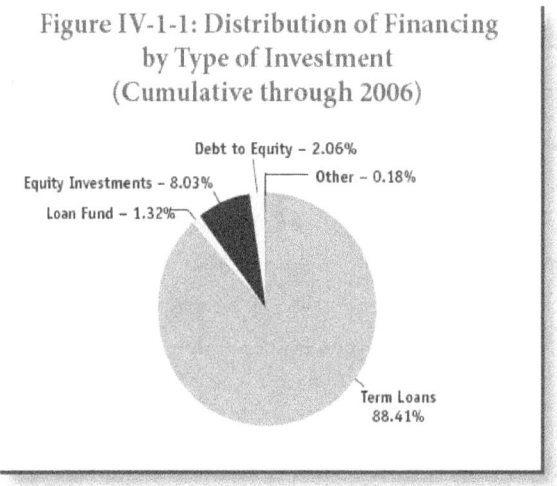

Figure IV-1-1: Distribution of Financing by Type of Investment (Cumulative through 2006)

Table IV-1-7 provides further detail on the number of transactions and average investment by type of investment. Term loans are not only the largest form of investment in total but are also the largest on average (with the exception of the two "other" investments) at $3.8 million per loan.

Table IV-1-7: Financing by Type of Investment (Cumulative through 2006)

Transaction Type	Transactions	Percent of Transactions	Amount	Percent of Dollars	Average
Term Loans	1,256	85.15%	4,816,798,008	88.41%	3,835,030
Lines of Credit	22	1.49%	71,756,313	1.32%	3,261,651
Equity Investments	150	10.17%	437,415,258	8.03%	2,916,102
Debt to Equity	45	3.05%	112,084,686	2.06%	2,490,771
Other	2	0.14%	10,000,000	0.18%	5,000,000
Total	1,475	100.00%	5,448,054,264	100.00%	3,693,596

Rates and Terms

Through the competitive application process, CDEs are asked about their plan to pass at least part of the economic benefit of the tax credit on to their borrowers and investees in the form of better rates and terms, as compared to standard market terms. Below is the complete list of what the CDFI Fund has characterized as better rates and terms:

- Equity Investments

- Equity-equivalent terms and conditions

- Debt with equity features

- Subordinated debt

- Longer than standard amortization period

- Lower than standard origination fees

- Below market interest rates

- Longer than standard period of interest-only payments

- More flexible borrower credit standards

- Non-traditional forms of collateral

- Lower than standard debt service coverage ratio

- Higher than standard loan to value ratio

- Loan loss reserve requirements that are less than standard

Over 98% of the QLICIs (1,452 out of 1,475) provided financing with features that satisfied one or more of the above-listed criteria. The most common features were below market interest rates on loans (83%), lower than standard origination fees (59%), and/or longer than standard amortization period (47%). See Figure IV-1-2 for details.

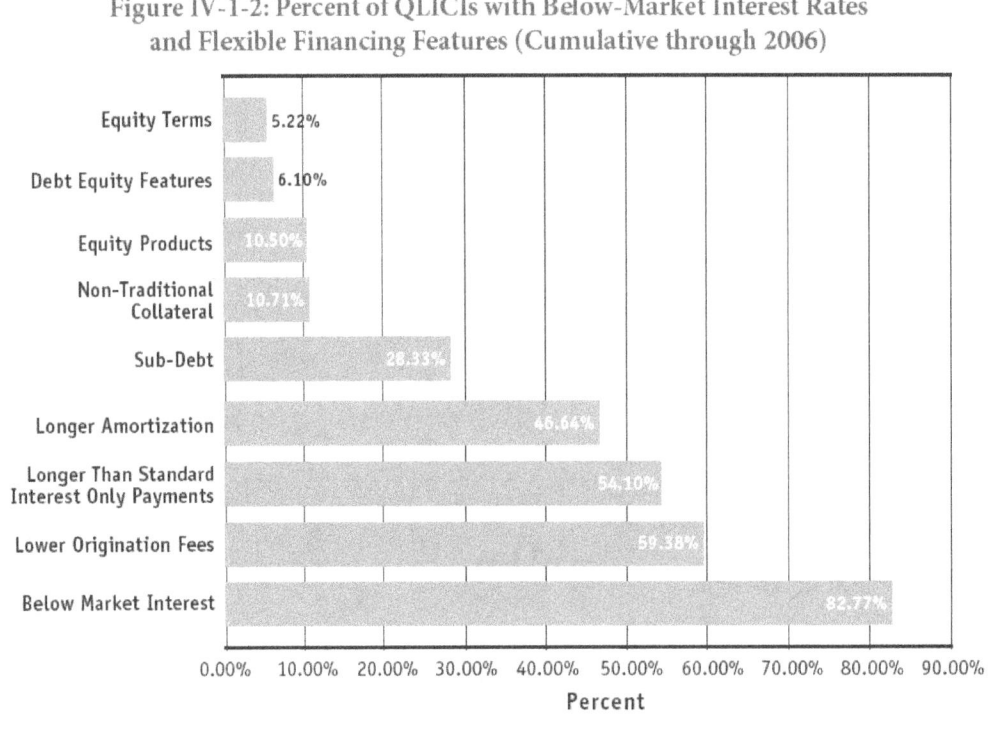

Figure IV-1-2: Percent of QLICIs with Below-Market Interest Rates
and Flexible Financing Features (Cumulative through 2006)

Figure IV-1-3 examines the rates and terms offered in transactions in Metropolitan areas versus those in Non-Metropolitan areas.[16] Transactions in the two areas generally offer the same features to investees. Over 80 percent of transactions in both areas offer below market interest rates, nearly 60 percent offer lower origination fees, and just over 45 percent offer a longer than standard amortization period. Differences are more apparent in the features that are relatively rare in both areas. Almost twice as many transactions take the form of subordinated debt in Metropolitan counties as in Non-Metropolitan counties (30 percent and 17 percent, respectively). Equity products are offered in 12 percent of Metropolitan county transactions, but only 3 percent of Non-Metropolitan county transactions. Similarly, equity-like terms are offered in 6 percent of transactions in Metropolitan counties but in only 0.5 percent of transactions in Non-Metropolitan counties.

---

[16]Transactions that could not be determined by type of area are not included.

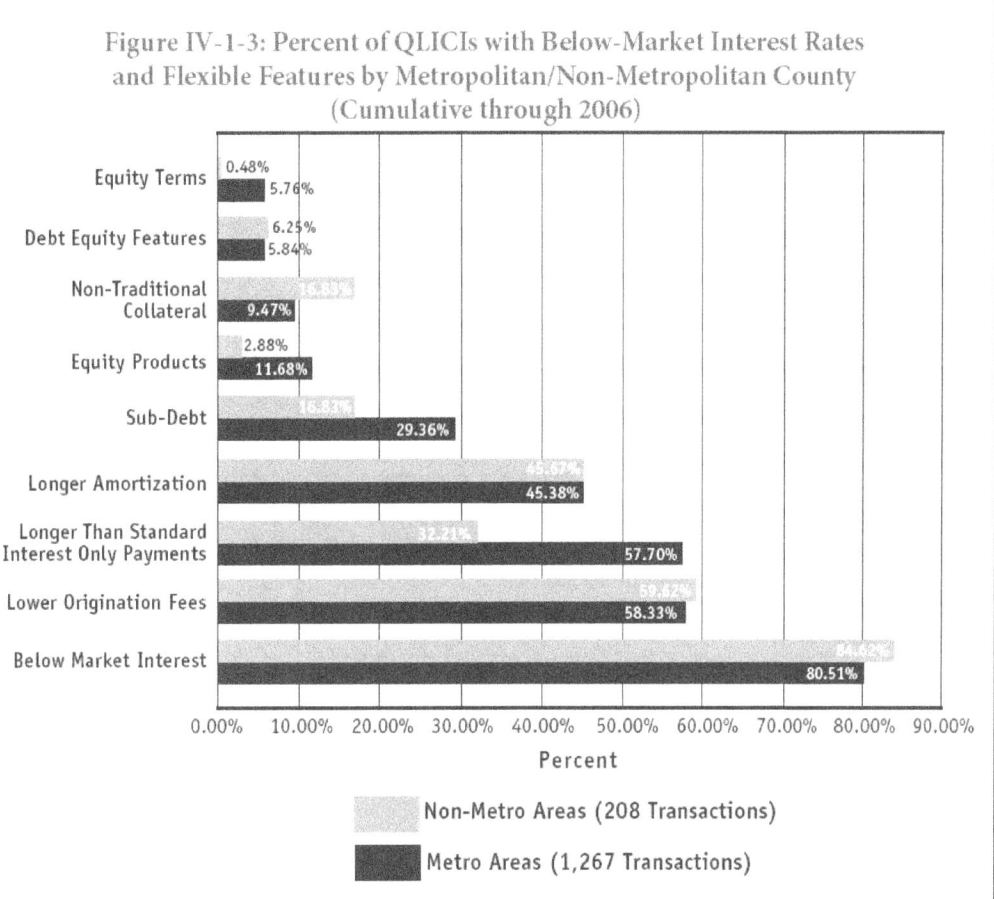

Figure IV-1-3: Percent of QLICIs with Below-Market Interest Rates
and Flexible Features by Metropolitan/Non-Metropolitan County
(Cumulative through 2006)

In the initial Rounds of the NMTC Program, the CDFI Fund did not require allocatees that reported particular financing features to provide a comparable marketplace standard (this feature has since been added to CIIS). Therefore, it is not possible, for the data provided, to determine how much better the rates or terms provided were from what was otherwise available. However, the available data appear to indicate that the difference may be substantial. For example, as shown in Table IV-1-8, among QLICIs in the form of below-market loans, rates were reported to average 4.8 percent for 1,196 loans. Among QLICIs in the form of loans which were not reported to be below market (129 loans), the average rate was 8.2 percent. This translates into an average savings of over 40 percent in interest costs.

Table IV-1-8: Interest Rates Comparison for QLICIs
in the Form of Loans by QALICB Type
(Cumulative through 2006)

	Below Market Rate		Absolute Difference (percentage points)	Percent Difference
	No	Yes		
Non-Real Estate QALICBs				
Mean	9.96%	5.20%	4.76	-47.79%
Median	8.86%	5.57%	3.29	-37.13%
Number of Loans	58	621		
Real Estate QALICBs				
Mean	6.69%	4.40%	2.29	-34.23%
Median	7.38%	4.91%	2.47	-33.47%
Number of Loans	71	579		
All QALICBs				
Mean	8.16%	4.81%	3.35	-41.05%
Median	7.75%	5.18%	2.57	-33.16%
Number of Loans	129	1,196		

Amortization Schedules

Table IV-1-9 displays information on the length and amortization schedule of QALICB investments. As expected, given the seven-year compliance period of the NMTC Program, most debt and debt-like investments (74.7 percent by number) have terms of seven years or more. Furthermore, only 15.5 percent of QALICB investments (about 19 percent of debt and debt-like investments) fully amortize over the life of the investment. Almost 66 percent of all investments (81 percent of debt and debt-like investments) have less than full amortization. Partially amortizing investments will have a reduced principal payment remaining at maturity while non-amortizing investments will pay only interest over the life of the investment with a full principal repayment at maturity.

Table IV-1-9: Length and Amortization Schedule of Financing
(Cumulative through 2006)

Term (Debt and Debt-like Investments)	Transactions	Percent
Less than 7 Years	223	15.12%
7 Years or More	1,102	74.71%
No Term (Equity Investments)	150	10.17%
Total	1,475	100.00%
Schedule (Debt and Debt-like Investments)	Transactions	Percent
Full Amortization	229	15.53%
Partial Amortization	388	26.31%
Non Amortization	583	39.53%
Other/ No Answer	125	8.47%
No Schedule (Equity Investments)	150	10.17%
Total	1,475	100.00%

IV-2: QLICI STATISTICAL DATA

As discussed in Section IV-1, through 2006, CDE allocatees have provided 1,475 loans and equity investments to QALICBs, totaling over $5.4 billion. These 1,475 transactions supported 1,131 projects.[17] The analysis in Section IV-2 focuses on this project-level data.

The 1,131 projects were split nearly evenly between real estate and non-real estate QALICBs. While most projects (920) were financed by a single loan or equity investment from an allocatee, 211 projects were financed by two or more investments, and one project was financed by nine separate transactions. See Table IV-2-1 for details.

---

[17] A transaction is an individual loan or investment, while a project includes all of the loans or investments provided to a QALICB by a single, distinct CDE or CDEs. For example, a QALICB may receive two loans and an equity investment from a CDE to develop a shopping center. This one investment (the shopping center) has three transactions (two loans and one equity investment) associated with it. Note that multiple CDEs can invest in a single investment. Prior to version 6.0 of the CIIS data system, the reporting system lacked detailed information on CDEs' disbursements at the project level to permit disaggregation of separate investments in joint projects. As a result, a certain amount of double-counting was unavoidable. This problem is rectified in version 6.0 of CIIS.

Table IV-2-1: QLICIs per Project
(Cumulative through 2006)

Transactions per Project	Non-Real Estate QALICBs	Real Estate QALICBs	Total
1	495	425	920
2	61	84	145
3	13	23	36
4	6	7	13
5	1	6	7
6	1	3	4
7	2	1	3
8	1	1	2
9	1	0	1
Total Projects	581	550	1,131

Projects in Areas of Higher Distress

An NMTC eligible low-income community is defined as a census tract with a poverty rate of not less than 20 percent or a median family income not greater than 80 percent of the area median family income. As noted in Section II of this report, in an effort to promote greater community impact, the CFDI Fund structured the NMTC allocation competition to reward those CDEs that commit to investing in projects located in areas of greater economic distress. These distress indicators as formulated for Round 5 were listed previously in this report.

As noted in Section II of the report, virtually all of the successful applicants indicated that they planned to serve areas of higher distress. This section analyzes whether investments are in fact being directed to these specially targeted communities. CDE data show that through the end of 2006 about 95 percent of QLICIs (1,072 out of 1,131) are located in designated areas of higher distress. Overall, about 75 percent of investments were directed to areas characterized by one or more of the following conditions: unemployment greater than 1.5x the national average, poverty rates in excess of 30 percent, or median income of 60 percent or less of area median income. As shown in Figure IV-2-1, more than 50 percent of the transactions are located in areas with median incomes of less than 60 percent of area median income. More than 40 percent went to areas with poverty rates greater than 30 percent. More than half of investments were in areas of significant unemployment. Relatively few transactions are located in areas designated as Native American or Hope VI (1.77 percent and 2.48 percent respectively).

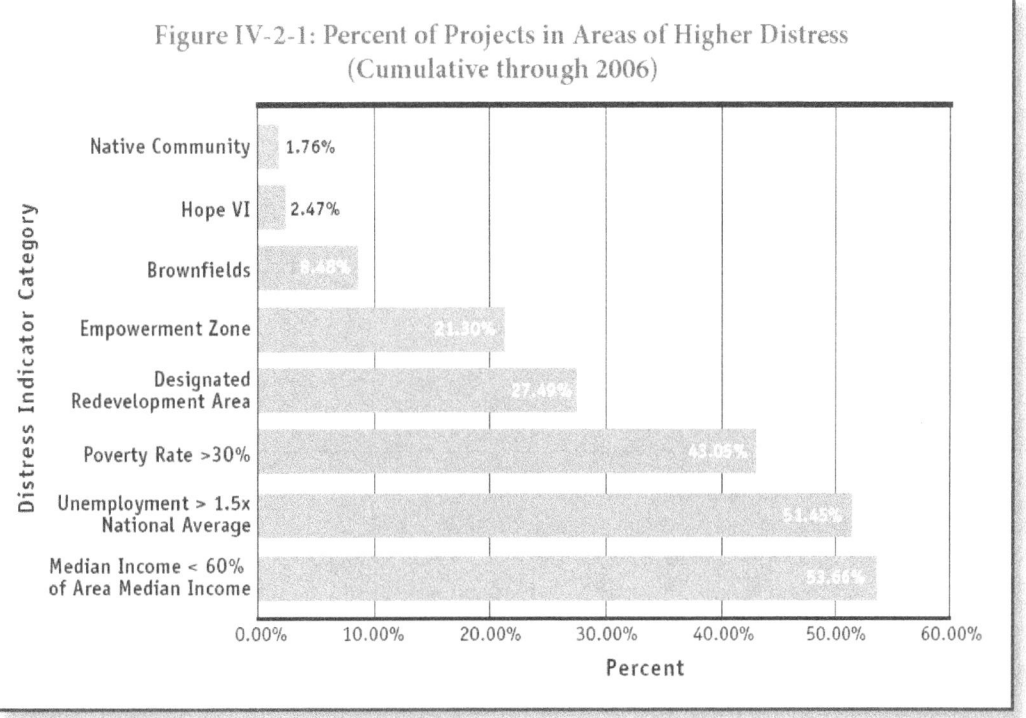

Figure IV-2-1: Percent of Projects in Areas of Higher Distress
(Cumulative through 2006)

Location of NTMC-Financed Transactions

NMTC-financed projects are located across the country in 47 states, the District of Columbia and Puerto Rico. They are included in all four US Census regions (Northeast, South, Midwest and West). Through 2006, Kansas, South Dakota, and Vermont were the only states not to have any NMTC-financed projects. Table IV-2-2 shows the top ten states with the largest dollar amounts of NMTC financed projects. Here, the dollar amount is the dollars invested (QLICIs), not the total project cost, which may be considerably higher.

Table IV-2-2: States with the Largest Dollar Amounts of NMTC-Financed Investment
(Cumulative through 2006)

State	Number of Projects	Investment Amount	Percent of Dollars	Average Investment Amount
NY	92	559,238,038	10.26%	6,078,674
CA	135	534,052,981	9.80%	3,955,948
OH	124	323,670,287	5.94%	2,610,244
MA	110	246,516,791	4.52%	2,241,062
OR	47	241,918,104	4.44%	5,147,194
WI	98	227,000,496	4.17%	2,316,332
WA	45	219,340,780	4.03%	4,874,240
KY	51	199,677,114	3.67%	3,915,238
MO	46	186,673,871	3.43%	4,058,128
NC	29	186,209,750	3.42%	6,421,026

Figure IV-2-2 is a national map showing total NMTC investment by state. Investment dollars are reasonably well distributed. The correlation coefficient between total investment dollars and population is 0.65, which means that states with higher populations tend to also have higher amounts of NMTC investments deployed within the state.[18] Over half the states have $100 million or less in total NMTC investment dollars.

---

[18] Population data were obtained from the Census Bureau web site, document NST-EST2007-1, downloaded March 11, 2008. Correlation coefficient is between investment dollars and population as of July 1, 2007.

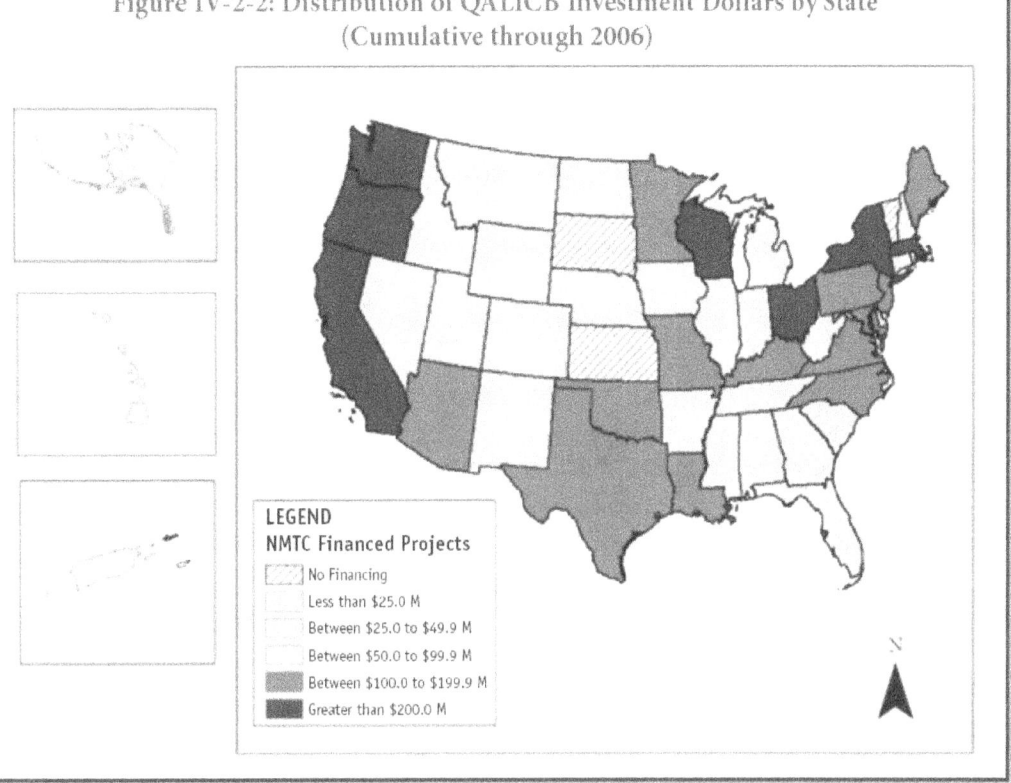

Figure IV-2-2: Distribution of QALICB Investment Dollars by State
(Cumulative through 2006)

LEGEND
NMTC Financed Projects
No Financing
Less than $25.0 M
Between $25.0 to $49.9 M
Between $50.0 to $99.9 M
Between $100.0 to $199.9 M
Greater than $200.0 M

Benefits to the Community

The CDFI Fund collects community impact data on a voluntary basis. The CDFI Fund did not validate the accuracy of this data, so reporting errors may exist. Table IV-2-3 summarizes the data provided to the CDFI Fund: median jobs created, median capacity of community facilities, and median square footage of real estate developed or rehabilitated.

The first section of Table IV-2-3 summarizes the number of jobs created as reported in the transaction level reports submitted by allocatees to the CDFI Fund. Projects can report on three types of jobs: construction jobs associated with the constructions of a NMTC-financed real estate project, permanent jobs associated with a business receiving NMTC-financed investment, and permanent jobs associated with businesses that are tenants in a NMTC-financed real estate project. The table shows 466 projects reported creating construction jobs, with a median of 80 jobs created among those projects. Three-hundred twenty projects reported that jobs were created or maintained at tenant businesses occupying NMTC-financed real estate, with a median of 80 jobs. Two-hundred thirty-three projects reported jobs created

or maintained at businesses receiving direct NMTC-financed investment. For these projects, the median number of jobs created or maintained was 16.

The second section of the table summarizes the type, number and capacity of community facilities created in terms of clients served. The CDFI Fund requests information on the type and capacity of arts centers, child care facilities, educational facilities, healthcare facilities, and "other" facilities. The "Other" category shows the largest number of projects (42) and shows a median capacity created of 1,641 slots. An additional 32 educational facilities (usually charter schools) have been constructed with a median capacity of 462 student-seats. Similarly, 18 health care facilities have been constructed, with a median capacity of 3,536 patients. Median project costs when disaggregated among community facility type ranges between $4.5 and $20 million.

The third section of the table summarizes the square footage of space created by NMTC-financed projects. Only 74 projects report creating manufacturing space, but these projects are generally larger, with median space created of 52,500 square feet. More projects report creating office and retail space (368 and 302 projects, respectively). Office projects have median square footage of over 23,000, while retail projects report a median of almost 25,000 square feet. Of course, a single project can create space for all three kinds of facilities. Median project costs vary between $4.5 and $12.6 million.

Table IV-2-3: Community Impact Data (Cumulative through 2006)

Jobs Creation Impacts	Construction	Businesses Financed	Tenant Businesses		
Number of Projects Reporting	466	233	320		
Median Number of Jobs Created	80	16	80		
Median Project Cost	$12,271,743	$2,138,133	$12,000,000		
Community Facilities Capacity Impacts	Arts Center	Childcare	Educational	Healthcare	Other
Number of Projects Reporting	26	15	42	18	44
Median Size of Facility					
Client Served	800	85	462	3,536	1,641
Median Project Cost	$20,385,384	$4,580,029	$12,608,705	$7,588,732	$10,720,494
Real Estate Impacts Square Footage	Manufacturing	Office	Retail		
Number of Projects Reporting	74	368	302		
Median Square Footage Created	52,500	23,271	24,613		
Median Project Cost	$4,455,000	$9,000,000	$12,634,903		

Total Project Costs

Investments by CDEs regularly finance only a portion of project costs. Data on both the amount of the QALICB investment and total project costs are collected in CIIS. Through the initial four years of data collection for the NMTC Program, this project cost data field was optional, not mandatory (the requirements for data submissions have since been changed to make this a mandatory field). Through 2006, a total of 904 projects (approximately 80% of the 1131 total projects) reported this data in CIIS. The result of this analysis is shown in Table IV-2-4.

Overall, CDE investments comprise less than a third of the total project investment (28.1%); for business and commercial real estate projects, the CDE proportion of the total investment is nearly 31% of total project costs, and in residential real estate projects CDE loans or investment represent nearly 37% of the total project costs.

Table IV-2-4: Total Project Financing By Purpose, QALICBs Only
(Cumulative through 2006)

Purpose	Number of Projects Reporting Data	Total Project ($)	NMTC Financing ($)	NMTC Proportion of Total Project Costs
Business Lending	257	2,950,935,976	909,001,591	30.8%
Commercial Real Estate	599	11,900,576,328	3,680,628,862	30.9%
Residential Real Estate	19	241,933,532	89,359,589	36.9%
Other	29	1,953,098,467	108,278,775	5.5%
Projects Reporting Data	904	17,046,544,303	4,787,268,816	28.1%

As indicated in Table IV-2-4, NMTC investments often represent only a portion of the capital investment in projects. Based upon the information presented through these 904 projects, each $1 of NMTC investment supports, on average, a total of $3.56 in total project costs. The total cost of a $1 NMTC investment to the Federal government, as measured by foregone tax revenues, is approximately 25 cents.[19] Thus, for a cost of 25 cents to the federal government, NMTCs support, on average, investments totaling $3.56 – or a ratio of over $14 for each $1 of foregone tax revenue ($3.56/$0.25 = 14.24).

---

[19] The cost basis of the investment is reduced by the amount of the credits claimed. Therefore, the investor pays taxes (generally at a corporate tax rate of 35%) on the 39 cents of credits claimed, which reduces the cost of the credit to the Federal government from 39 cents to approximately 25 cents [.39 * (1-.35) = .2535].

Project Cost in Metropolitan and Non-Metropolitan Counties

Table IV-2-5 shows project cost data among Metropolitan and Non-Metropolitan counties for non-real estate QALICBs and real estate QALICBs. Note that, of the 1,131 projects, only 904 provided information on project cost. Almost 86 percent of the reporting projects are located in Metropolitan counties, and they account for almost 89 percent of total project costs. They tend to be more expensive; on average, project costs in Metropolitan counties ($20 million) are higher than Non-Metropolitan counties ($12.5 million). Interestingly, the relative costs of projects funded by real estate and non-real estate QALICBs differ between Metropolitan and Non-Metropolitan counties. In Metropolitan counties, project costs for real estate QALICBs average $28 million, while project costs for non-real estate QALICBs average about $8 million. In contrast, project costs for non-real estate QALICBs in Non-Metropolitan counties average $14.0 million, while project costs for real estate QALICBs are under $5 million on average.

Table IV-2-5: Project Cost by Purpose
(Cumulative through 2006)

	Metropolitan Counties			Non-Metropolitan Counties		
	Number of Projects	Amount ($)	Average ($)	Number of Projects	Amount ($)	Average ($)
Non-Real Estate	311	2,543,546,517	8,178,606	106	1,486,306,236	14,021,757
Real Estate	465	12,909,227,831	27,761,780	22	107,463,718	4,884,714
Total	776	15,452,774,348	19,913,369	128	1,593,769,954	12,451,328

Conclusion

In a relatively short period of time the New Markets Tax Credit Program has became an important tool for facilitating the investment of private sector capital in low-income communities. The summary findings in this report indicate that, among other things:

- NMTC investments are being made in communities with significantly higher levels of distress than are minimally required under program rules.

- There is a strong demand for tax credit allocations.

- Community Development Entities have been successful in securing investor capital.

- The NMTC Program is fostering new investor relationships.

- Virtually all NMTC product offerings include non-traditional rates and terms to the borrowers, including below market interest rates, lower origination fees and longer than standard periods of interest-only payments.

- The NTMC Program is tremendously cost effective in using federal tax credits to induce investments in projects in low-income communities.

The CDFI Fund will to continue to collect data from program participants and monitor and report on trends as the program matures.

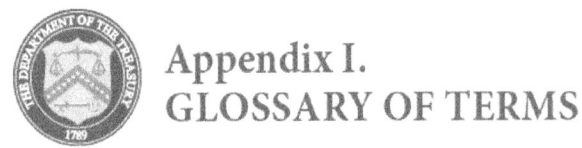

Appendix I.
GLOSSARY OF TERMS

Allocatee
An *applicant* that receives a *NMTC allocation*.

Allocation Agreement
An agreement to be entered into by the CDFI Fund and a CDE, relating to the *NMTC allocation*, pursuant to IRC §45D(f)(2).

Applicant
Any legal entity that is applying to the CDFI Fund for the receipt of a *NMTC allocation*. This term includes any *Subsidiary* of the *applicant*, which may receive a transfer of all or part of a *NMTC allocation* from the *applicant*.

ATS Data
Allocation Tracking System

Community Development Entity (CDE)
Under IRC §45D(c)(1), any domestic corporation or partnership if:

(1) The primary mission of the entity is serving, or providing investment capital for, *low-Income communities* or *low-income persons*;

(2) The entity maintains accountability to residents of *Low-Income Communities* through their representation on any governing board of the entity or on an advisory board to the entity; and

(3) The entity is certified by the CDFI Fund as a CDE. *Specialized Small Business Investment Companies (SSBICs)* and *Community Development Financial Institutions (CDFIs)* are deemed to be CDEs in the manner set forth in Guidance published by the Fund (66 Federal Register 65806, December 20, 2001).

Community Development Financial Institution (CDFI)
An entity that has been certified by the CDFI Fund as meeting the criteria set forth in section 103 of the Community Development Banking and Financial Institutions Act of 1994 (12 U.S.C. 4702). For further details, refer to the CDFI Program regulations set forth at 12 CFR 1805.201.

Community Investment Impact System (CIIS)
A web-based data collection system that CDFIs and CDEs will use to submit their Institution-Level Reports and Transaction-Level Reports to the CDFI Fund.

Controlling Entity
An entity that controls an *applicant*.

Disadvantaged Business

A business that is (a) located in a *Low-Income Community*; or (b) is owned by a *Low-Income Person*; or (c) a business that has inadequate access to investment capital.

Disadvantaged Community

This term has the same meaning as a *Low-Income Community*.

Equity Investment

Under IRC §45D(b)(6) Equity Investment means any stock (other than nonqualified preferred stock as defined in IRC §351(g)(2)) in an entity that is a corporation and any capital interest in an entity that is a partnership.

Financial Counseling and Other Services

Advice provided by a *CDE* relating to the organization or operation of a trade or business. See 26 CFR 1.45D-1(d)(7).

Go-Zone

The Gulf Opportunity (GO) Zone Act of 2005 (Pub. L. No. 1109-135) defined businesses and targeted populations affected by Hurricane Katrina that eligible for certain federal assistance, including application to the NMTC program.

Low-Income Community

Under IRC §45D(e)(1), any population census tract if:

(1) The poverty rate for such tract is at least 20 percent, or

(2) (a) In the case of a tract not located within a Metropolitan area, the median family income for such tract does not exceed 80 percent of statewide median family income, or (b) in the case of a tract located within a Metropolitan area, the median family income for such tract does not exceed 80 percent of the greater of statewide median family income or the Metropolitan area median family income.

With respect to IRC §45D(e)(1)(B), possession-wide median family income shall be used (in lieu of statewide income) in assessing the status of census tracts located within a possession of the United States.

Under IRC §45D(e)(2), *Targeted Populations* will also be treated as *Low-Income Communities*.
See IRS Notice 2006-60.

Under IRC §45D(e)(3), in the case of an area that is not tracted for population census tracts, the equivalent county divisions (as defined by the Bureau of the Census for purposes of determining poverty areas) shall be used for purposes of defining poverty rates and median family incomes. See IRC §45D(e) for additional criteria.

Low-Income Person

Any individual having an income, adjusted for family size, of not more than:

(1) For Metropolitan areas, 80 percent of the area median family income; and

(2) For Non-Metropolitan areas, the greater of (a) 80 percent of the area median family income or (b) 80 percent of the statewide Non-Metropolitan area median family income.

Minority-Owned or Controlled

A business that is more than 50% owned or controlled by one or more persons who are members of minority ethnic group. If the business is a for-profit concern, more than 50% of its owners must be minorities; if the business is a non-profit concern, more than 50% of its board of directors must be minorities (or its Chief Executive Officer, Executive Director, General Partner or Managing Member must be a minority).

New Markets Venture Capital Company (NMVCC)

An entity designated as a NMVCC by the Small Business Administration under the New Markets Venture Capital Company Program.

NMTC Allocation

An allocation of tax credit authority pursuant to the New Markets Tax Credit Program.

Qualified Active Low-Income Community Business (QALICB)

Under IRC §45D(d)(2), any corporation (including a non-profit corporation) or partnership if for any taxable year:

(1) At least 50 percent of total gross income of such entity is derived from the active conduct of a qualified business within any *Low-Income Community*;

(2) A substantial portion of the use of the tangible property of such entity (whether owned or leased) is within any *Low-Income Community*;

(3) A substantial portion of the services performed for such entity by its employees are performed in any *Low-Income Community*;

(4) Less than 5 percent of the average of the aggregate unadjusted bases of the property of such entity is attributable to collectibles (as defined in IRC §408(m)(2)) other than collectibles that are held primarily for sale to customers in the ordinary course of such business; and

(5) Less than 5 percent of the average of the aggregate unadjusted bases of the property of such entity is attributable to nonqualified financial property (as defined in IRC §1397C(e)).

Qualified Equity Investment (QEI)

Under IRC §45D(b)(1), any *Equity Investment* in a CDE if:

(1) Such investment is acquired by the investor at its original issue (directly or through an underwriter) solely in exchange for cash;

(2) Substantially all of such cash is used by the *CDE* to make *QLICIs*; and

(3) The investment is designated for purposes of IRC §45D by the *CDE* as a QEI. QEI also includes an *Equity Investment* purchased from a prior holder, to the extent provided in IRC §45D(b)(4).

QEI does not include any *Equity Investment* issued by a CDE more than five years after the date the CDE receives a *NMTC Allocation*. Please refer to the *NMTC Program Income Tax Regulations* at 26 CFR 1.45D-1(c) and related Internal Revenue Service notices for more information.

Qualified Low-Income Community Investments (QLICI)

Under IRC §45D(d)(1), a *QLICI* is:

(1) Any capital or *Equity Investment* in, or loan to, any *QALICB* (as defined in IRC§45D(d)(2));

(2) The purchase from a CDE of any loan made by such entity that is a *QLICI*;

(3) *Financial Counseling and Other Services* to businesses located in, and residents of, *Low-Income Communities*; and

(4) Any *Equity Investment* in, or loan to, any *CDE*.

Small Business Investment Company (SBIC)

An entity defined in 15 USC 662(3).

Specialized Small Business Investment Company (SSBIC)

An entity defined in IRC §1044(c)(3).

Targeted Population

As defined in 12 U.S.C. 4702(20) and 12 C.F.R. 1805.201, the term "targeted population" means individuals, or an identifiable group of individuals, including an Indian Tribe, who (A) are *Low-Income Persons*; or (B) otherwise lack adequate access to loans or investments.

Appendix II. ANALYSIS OF SCORE DATA USING A DIFFERENCE OF MEANS TEST

Score data has been analyzed using a means test. This test assesses whether the means of two groups (in this case the scores of applications from CDFIs, banks, or non-profits, for instance, in contrast to the scores of all other applicants) are statistically different from each other. It is not a test that simply examines the means of two samples, but additionally calculates the standard deviation and the distribution of all standard errors across the entire range of these two variables. It is standard practice in statistics to begin with the assumption that there is no statistically significant difference between two means—the differences are simply a result of chance. The test employed for this analysis calculates the mean of the two variables, the distribution of the standard errors, and then, depending on the number of cases, provides a statistic showing the probability of whether a difference in means between two groups is a true difference as opposed to simply a result of chance. The probabilities shown in Table A-1 should be read as the likelihood that the observed differences between two variables are or are not the result of chance.

For example, in round 2 banks and publicly-traded companies scored an average of 50.9 on the business strategy section while non-profits scored a mean of 44.9. The overall mean score for this section for this round was 44.9. The difference between the banks and publicly-traded companies business strategy score and all applicants is 6.0 whereas the same measure between the average scores on the business section and the overall score is only 0.1. However, are these differences statistically significant? In statistical analysis, it is standard to only accept this difference if it is *unlikely* to have occurred by chance. In this study, a difference of means is accepted as truly being different if the probability that the difference is the result of chance is 5% or less which is represented mathematically as $p < .05$. (A 5% test is a common yardstick in the social sciences.) In the example used here, observed differences of means are ruled to be not the result of chance if $p < .05$. For the means test of the business strategy scores of banks and publicly-traded companies and all other applicants, the test results in $p < .0001$; the comparable statistic for non-profits is $p < .838$. Therefore, the difference between the banks business strategy score and other applicants is statistically significant because the observed difference is unlikely to have occurred by chance. In contrast, the difference in the mean score for non-profits and that of all other applicants in this round is not accepted as statistically significant because this difference is likely to have occurred by chance 83.8% of the time.

Table A-I presents the results of this analysis. Each entry in the table shows the significance of the means test between the mean score for each section of the NMTC application by applicant type versus the mean section scores all other applicants. For example, in the test of the Round 2 business strategy scores for certified CDFIs vs. all others, the significance is $p < .0021$, indicating that certified CDFIs scored higher than other applicants in the business strategy section and that the difference in means is unlikely to be the result of chance. Similarly, non-profits scored higher than other applicants on the community impact section in Round 4 than other applicants—the significance was $p < .0021$.

In general, thrifts, banks, and bank holding and publicly-traded companies score significantly higher than entities that are not thrifts, banks, or bank holding or publicly-traded companies. Certified CDFIs score significantly higher than entities that are not certified CDFIs in their business strategy plans and their management capacity and community impact, but interestingly in Round 5 only the community impact score was statistically significantly higher. There are almost no statistical differences between the scores of government controlled entities and other entities.

Table A-I: Significance Tests of Scoring by Applicant Type and Round

	Business	Capital	Community	Management
Thrift, Bank, or Bank Holding Company and Publicly-traded Companies				
Round 2	0.0001	0.0001	0.0268	0.0001
Round 3	0.0408	0.0205	0.6496	0.0582
Round 4	0.0001	0.0001	0.0081	0.0001
Round 5	0.0327	0.0001	0.1252	0.0005
Certified CDFI				
Round 2	0.0021	0.6101	0.0002	0.0030
Round 3	0.0001	0.1680	0.0001	0.0012
Round 4	0.0001	0.5405	0.0001	0.0059
Round 5	0.1898	0.7583	0.0041	0.1712
Non-Profits				
Round 2	0.8978	0.0036	0.2987	0.5441
Round 3	0.9071	0.0822	0.0838	0.4475
Round 4	0.0856	0.6108	0.0021	0.6858
Round 5	0.4666	0.0567	0.7665	0.1134
Government Controlled Entity				
Round 2	0.0230	0.0858	0.0514	0.0223
Round 3	0.8575	0.8680	0.3242	0.8367
Round 4	0.7998	0.5951	0.6074	0.0941
Round 5	0.2189	0.8190	0.1116	0.9616

CommunityDevelopment
Financial Institutions Fund

UNITED STATES DEPARTMENT OF THE TREASURY

VISIT THE FUND AT:
www.cdfifund.gov

www.ingramcontent.com/pod-product-compliance
Lightning Source LLC
Chambersburg PA
CBHW080616290526
45790CB00007B/2800